D0590719

# CRICKET
## ONE LINERS

First published in Great Britain in 2003
by PAST TIMES®, Oxford, England


Copyright © 2003 Complete Editions

Designed by seagulls
Printed in Thailand by Imago
Illustrations from the Beryl Peters Archive

# PAST TIMES®

# *The Game*

Life is just an elaborate metaphor for cricket.
MARVIN COHEN

What do they know of cricket
who only cricket know?
C.L.R. JAMES

In a sense cricket is – US.
H.A. VACHELL

I think it's the most marvellous,
witty and amusing game.
MICHAEL CHARLTON

Over the origins and context of village cricket the
chronicler must hover warily, for its image exists as
much in the common imagination as in actuality.
RONALD MASON

It is hard to tell where the MCC ends and the
Church of England begins.
J.B. PRIESTLEY

It can be as brutal as rugby
and as delicate as chess . . .
H.R.H. PRINCE PHILIP, DUKE OF EDINBURGH

*It's more than a game.
It's an institution.* THOMAS HUGHES

# *Personally, I have always looked upon cricket as organized loafing.*

WILLIAM TEMPLE

Here is a game so doggedly peculiar
and dangerous that no foreign nations …
have ever adopted it.
PETER USTINOV

If the French noblesse had been capable of playing
cricket with their peasants, their châteaux
would never have been burnt.
G.M. TREVELYAN

Cricket is first and foremost a dramatic spectacle.
C.L.R. JAMES

Cricket, golf, hockey, all had a common ancestry in
which a ball was struck by a wooden implement.
But the particular ancestor of cricket was – cricket.
ERIC PARKER

There is one great similarity between music and
cricket – there are slow movements in each.
NEVILLE CARDUS

# *Bowling is as important a feature of the game of cricket as batting.* SIR PELHAM WARNER

A good game of cricket, contested between teams whose players are of roughly equal ability, is as intricate as any war.
JOHN GRANT

But how perfect in its own way is cricket …
It is a game which keeps boys out of mischief.
PROFESSOR CASE

There is only one thing in criket and that is the strate bat. Keep yore bat strate boy and all will be all right in life as in criket.
GEOFFREY WILLANS & RONALD SEARLE

Village cricket is not what it was but nothing is.
JOHN ARLOTT 1977

Cricket? I thought it was an English food.
ALEX METREVELI

This isn't no time for playin' the fool
nor makin' no sport: this is cricket!
EDWARD KAMAU BRATHWAITE

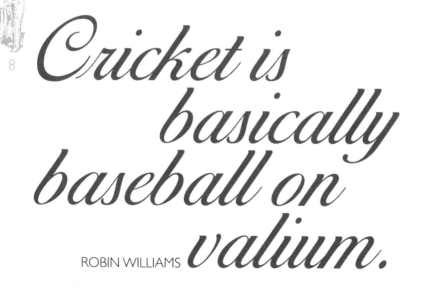

*Cricket is basically baseball on valium.*

ROBIN WILLIAMS

Cricket? It civilises people and creates
good gentlemen. I want everyone to play
cricket in Zimbabwe. I want ours to
be a nation of gentlemen.

ROBERT MUGABE

# *Cricket is the pride and privilege of the Englishman alone.*

JOHN MITFORD

... the whole thing bears a closer resemblance
to Wellington's campaign in the Peninsular War
to so many 'flannelled fools' amusing
themselves in the sun.
H.R.H. PRINCE PHILIP, DUKE OF EDINBURGH

Who would think that a little bit of leather and
two pieces of wood, had such a delightful and
delighting power!
MARY RUSSELL MITFORD

Cricket is my wife.
DICKIE BIRD

Cricket is an altogether too sacred thing to him to
be tampered with on merely religious grounds.
H.G. WELLS

Sunday League Cricket – multi-coloured
pyjamas, two-tone umpires and white balls
with black seams. There is nothing like
traditional English sport.
DAVID HUNN

*Cricket
is to me
summer, and
summer cricket.*
LORD HARRIS

*Cricket is not only a game, but a school of the greatest social importance.* LORD HARRIS

It takes up much time, which the modern
world would like to turn into money . . .
I like the fact that it is not modern.
SIMON RAVEN

It would be nice if there was more pride
put back into English cricket by having people
wearing caps, like the Australians do.
JOHN KETTLEY

As the greatest of all team games, the accent in
cricket is on the team rather than on the individual.
E.W. SWANTON

The combination of Britisher and Sunshine spells cricket – or so, at least, it seems to one who has travelled many thousands of miles.

SIR PELHAM WARNER

Coarse cricket, which is often seen but seldom believed . . . is a sport more remarkable for the enthusiasm than for the aptitude of its players and is best played against breweries.

SPIKE HUGHES

13

There is a widely-held and quite erroneous
belief that cricket is just another game.
H.R.H. PRINCE PHILIP, DUKE OF EDINBURGH

No two games are ever identical . . . because of
factors such as the size of the ground, the weather,
individual performances, the state and size of the
pitch, the toss, Mrs Jones' Dundee cake, and the
sum the opposition have offered the umpires.
JOHN GRANT

14

*Many continentals
think life is a game,
the English think
cricket is a game.*
GEORGE MIKES

*That's what cricket is all about. Two batsmen pitting their wits against one another.* FRED TRUEMAN

Cricket has done more to consolidate
the Empire than any other influence.
LORD HARRIS

I tend to believe that cricket is the greatest
thing that God ever created on Earth.
HAROLD PINTER

Hail Cricket! glorious, manly, British Game!
First of all Sports! be first alike in Fame.
JAMES LOVE

In short ... English cricket needs
an injection of culture and enterprise.
JOHN WOODCOCK

Cricket is essentially English, and though our
countrymen carry it abroad wherever they go, it is
difficult to inoculate or knock it into the foreigner.
JOHN AYE

*One-day cricket is exhibition. Test cricket is examination.*

HENRY BLOFELD

# Those Who Play the Game

Every ball is for me the first ball.
DON BRADMAN

He's six feet tall, heavily built and has a
rolling gait, like a sailor who has just come
ashore, or a ploughman returning after
a long day tilling the soil.
BRIAN JOHNSTON ON GRAHAM GOOCH

They came to see me bat not to see you bowl.
W.G. GRACE ON REFUSING TO LEAVE THE CREASE
HAVING BEEN BOWLED OUT FIRST BALL

Perhaps the luckiest and certainly the happiest day
of my life – I bowled Australia out before lunch.
DIARY ENTRY OF FRANK TYSON, 5 JANUARY 1955

Like so many England teams we were slightly
arrogant and distinctly intolerant of the
accommodation provided and some of the
administration arrangements.
TREVOR BAILEY ON THE WEST INDIES TOUR OF 1954

I've noticed that every team of village
standard or below has a 'village blacksmith'.
The player concerned need not in fact be a
blacksmith – indeed, nowadays, he's almost
certainly not – but he has the build,
approach and philosophy of life of one.
JOHN GRANT

19

# When you play Test cricket you don't give Englishmen an inch.

DON BRADMAN

He was the first umpire to combine the distinct roles of top-flight umpire and music-hall comedian.

MATTHEW ENGEL ON DICKIE BIRD

It is strange, perhaps, but true, how many of us agreed on this: that we were never so thankful for having been cricketers as we were when we were guests of the Japanese.

MAJOR E.W. SWANTON, 1946

It is a fact not generally known that in her youth Queen Victoria had the makings of a cricketer of considerable stature.

PETER TINNISWOOD

We have always felt that the success, or otherwise, of county cricket, and the support of the public for it, lies in the hands of the county captains.
LETTER IN *THE TIMES*, 16 MAY 1946, SIGNED BY: H.K. FOSTER, W.L. FOSTER, B.S. FOSTER, G.N. FOSTER, N.J.A. FOSTER

*I couldn't bat for the length of time required scoring 500. I'd get bored and fall over.*

DENIS COMPTON ON BRIAN LARA'S RECORD-BREAKING SCORE.

21

It's a bit like saying that Romeo had a slight crush
on Juliet or Abelard had a fancy for Heloise.
MICHAEL PARKINSON ON HOW IT IS AN
UNDERSTATEMENT TO SAY THAT
DICKIE BIRD LOVES CRICKET

He loved to walk sideways towards
them, like a grimly playful crab.
R.C. ROBERTSON-GLASGOW ON GEORGE GUNN
APPROACHING FAST BOWLERS

The modern professional cricketer does not
get drunk at Lord's or often get a century
there, or anywhere else, before lunch.
NEVILLE CARDUS

*The Gentleman's Magazine* of September 1743
had an article … which adversely criticised the
game, for the reason, amongst others, that peer
and peasant joined together in the play.
ERIC PARKER

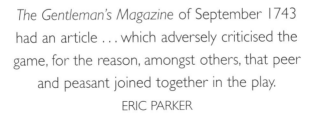

I broke my nose keeping wicket, which is why I have this rather handsome and eccentric profile.
ERIC IDLE

But he could do what W.G. never ventured to do, viz. cut balls off the middle and off stumps.
REV. R.S. HOLMES ON EPHRAIM LOCKWOOD

When I step across that boundary rope, I'm a different man. It's the only time I feel in total control.
DICKIE BIRD

*Compton is the axiom of tomorrow.* R.C. ROBERTSON-GLASGOW

I got the impression that the main reason
they'd come to Alderney was not to play
cricket particularly, but to meet John Arlott.
GEOFF RENNARD ON A VISITING TEAM OF
ABORIGINAL CRICKETERS, 1988


The first time you face up to a googly
you're going to be in trouble if you've
never faced one before.
TREVOR BAILEY

The not-outer is small, wizened, misanthropic,
drinks half-shandies and eats sparingly.
MICHAEL STEVENSON

Professionalism in a lawyer or engineer
is supposed to be an attribute, but when used
in a cricketing context the term somehow
insinuates indiscipline, boorishness – everything
in fact that is traditionally not cricket.
ASIF IQBAL

# *Rain and bad light have followed me around all my life.*

Every team is a hot-bed of personality
conflict where envy, jealousy and
ambition work against unity.
SUKHI TURNER

. . . when you're on the cricket pitch trifles such
as deep, inalienable hatred tend to be ignored.
JOHN GRANT

It stands to reason that cricket dominated
by amateurs must be livelier than cricket in
which professionals . . . set the tone.
SIR JOHN SQUIRE

For myself, I should like 100 balls to the over.
ALFRED MYNN

Playing against a team with Ian Chappell as a
captain turns a cricket match into gang warfare.
MIKE BREARLEY

To be a great fast bowler you 'ave
to 'ave a big 'eart and a big arse.
FRED TRUEMAN

The first decade of Major Tennyson's
[later Lord Tennyson] captaincy of Hampshire
was indeed gloriously uncertain.
ERIC PARKER

If I'm asked to play cricket hereafter,
I am wholly determined to scratch.
Life's void of all pleasure and laughter;
I bungled the easiest catch.
P.G. WODEHOUSE

28

If the England men's cricket team were
as good as the England girls' cricket
team, it might do much better.
IAIN SPROAT MP

*I was not a great cricketer,
but I captained the school
in a lean year.* LORD RUNCIE

*I can bowl so slowly that if I don't like the ball I can run after it and get it back.* J.M. BARRIE

Whatever the reason, to the real cricket-lover the deeds of W.G. Grace over a century ago, the batting of Victor Trumper in the 'twenties and the fast bowling of Harold Larwood in the 'thirties remain as vivid as the doings of the West Indians in England last summer.
KARL JOHNSTON

I guess I never had a chance, it was always going to be cricket, cricket, and just a little more cricket for good measure.
RICHARD HADLEE

Fred Trueman ... describes my bowling
as left arm blankety blank over the
wicket, which is very accurate.
LESLIE CROWTHER

But a Napoleon amongst cricket captains can do
nothing if the rank and file are disloyal, so that both
leader and follower have their part to play.
SIR PELHAM WARNER

In the end it is only the camaraderie of the
team, the lifelong friendships which you forge,
and the opportunity for interesting sorties
outside the grind of the cricket grounds
which make the experience worthwhile.
BILL O'REILLY

Both are fitting adornments and exponents
of a game that was meant not as an imitation of,
but as a refreshment from, the worldly struggle.
R.C. ROBERTSON-GLASGOW
ON DENIS COMPTON AND W.J. EDRICH

31

... you could guarantee that the kid with the
whitest shirt, the whitest trousers, the whitest boots
and pads, could not play cricket to save his life.

JIMMY TARBUCK

What I do is creak out to the square and hope to
plonk a little timber on the ball.
PETER O'TOOLE

I only ever think about cricket. I just worry that
when I pack up I'll be dead in twelve months.
DICKIE BIRD

The players are the ones who know how soul-
destroying it is to play professional cricket in front
of three men and a thermos.
LORD MACLAURIN

*...and Ray Illingworth
is relieving himself
in front of the
pavilion.*
JOHN ARLOTT

# I'm 60 next month, but I still regard myself as a *promising batsman.* HAROLD PINTER

To think of playing cricket for hard cash! Money
and gentility would ruin any pastime under the sun.
MARY RUSSELL MITFORD, 1823

What is human life but a game of cricket? And, if
so, why should not the ladies play it as well as we?
THE THIRD DUKE OF DORSET IN 1777

I was qualified for Surrey
in everything except talent.
JOHN MAJOR

There are good one-day players, there are good
Test players, and vice versa.
TREVOR BAILEY

Because Bradman will always be remembered is no
reason why Ponsford should be neglected; when
the sun rises it is a mistake to forget the moon.
R.C. ROBERTSON-GLASGOW

The last bowler to be knighted was Francis Drake.
ALEC BEDSER

He couldn't preach but we forgave him
because he played cricket.
ALISON UTTLEY ON A LOCAL VICAR

*It was a good tour
to break my teeth in.*
BERNARD THOMAS

# *A cricketer – a creature very nearly as stupid as a dog.*

BERNARD LEVIN

*If you cannot be a cricketer you can at least look like one.*

DON BRADMAN

He didn't quite manage to get his leg over.
JONATHAN AGNEW – ON AN UNSUCCESSFUL
ATTEMPT BY IAN BOTHAM TO STEP OVER THE WICKET

Test cricket's a duel of wits as much as anything,
and England's David Gower and I were, well,
trigger-happy about the first test at Lord's in 1986.
RICHARD HADLEE

My solution is to let the players drink
at the beginning of the game, not after.
It always works in our picnic matches.
PAUL HOGAN ON HOW TO BRIGHTEN UP CRICKET

Women playing cricket should treat it as a matter
between consenting friends in private.
MICHAEL PARKINSON

It has been said that good batsmen are
born and not made, but my experience
is rather to the contrary.
SIR PELHAM WARNER

Once in my heyday of cricket
Oh day I shall ever recall!
I captured that glorious wicket,
The greatest, the grandest of all.
ARTHUR CONAN DOYLE

37

He was the first who departed from the
custom of the old players before him, who
deemed it heresy to leave the crease for the ball;
he would get in at it, and hit it straight off and
straight on; and egad! it went as if it had been fired.
JOHN NYREN ON TOM SUETER

The last time I played in a village match
I was given out lbw first ball. That sort
of umpiring should be looked into.
H.R.H. PRINCE PHILIP, DUKE OF EDINBURGH

I am told that the flow of language from the
bowler was at once an education and a delight
to the young professionals on the side.
DOUG INSOLE ON TREVOR BAILEY

If the best spin bowler in the country
were a woman, what would be done
about the dressing-rooms at Lord's?
NEVILLE CARDUS

*If I could dream about
doing anything else, I
would be a fast bowler.*
PETER SCUDAMORE

# *I never play cricket. It requires one to assume such indecent postures.*

OSCAR WILDE

A steeple-high catch in the country begins
to lose its terrors when one has caught a dozen
such the evening before at field practice.

THE JUBILEE BOOK OF CRICKET

Neville Cardus once wrote of Woolley's off-drives
that they were like butterflies going into the flame.

JAMES AGATE

It would be well if matters could be so arranged
that great bowlers, without loss of income, were
enabled to conserve their energies for the summer.
C. STEWART CAINE ON THE SUBJECT OF
WINTER TOURS IN AUSTRALIA

... it is human to err, occasionally, even if
the gods have lavished on you a share of grace
and skill not given to ordinary mortals.
NEVILLE CARDUS ON GARY SOBERS

A captain's role is that of PR officer,
agricultural consultant, psychiatrist,
accountant, nursemaid and diplomat.
DOUG INSOLE

*I saw much better batsmen
than I was. Lots of them ...
they just kept getting out.*
DON BRADMAN

A good captain must be a fighter, confident but
not arrogant, firm but not obstinate, able to take
criticism without letting it unduly disturb him,
for he is sure to get it – and unfairly, too.
DON BRADMAN


No one regards Johnston [W.A. 'Bill' Johnston]
as other than a 'rabbit' as a batsman.
WISDEN

*It's a well-known fact that, when I'm on 99, I'm the best judge of a run in all the bloody world.*

ALAN WHARTON

You can't consider yourself established
as a cricketer until you have consumed
a ton of lettuce by May.
GARY SOBERS

It's less a matter of the sweet sound of
willow on leather and more one of the sound
of a rather sickly snick followed by screams
as the slips nurse their staved fingers.
ROY HATTERSLEY

One of the most beautiful sights that can be
imagined, and which would have delighted an artist,
was to see him make himself up to hit a ball.
JOHN NYREN ON WILLIAM BELDHAM

When he died I offered the thought that if they didn't
play cricket in heaven he would ask for a transfer . . .
MICHAEL PARKINSON ON HIS FATHER

I prefer a green where the stocks are still
standing, and I would rather not play at
all if there is no parish beadle.
FRED GALE

43

*A fast bowler is like
a dachsund: four short
legs and his balls swing
both ways.* BRIAN JOHNSTON

# Those Who Watch the Game

That slow motion replay doesn't
show how fast the ball was travelling.
RICHIE BENAUD

Say, when do they begin?
GROUCHO MARX

I do love cricket – it's so very English.
SARAH BERNHARDT ON SEEING A GAME OF FOOTBALL

The synthetic indignation of certain English
cricketers over alleged Pakistani ball tampering –
the unedifying in pursuit of the unbeatable.
PATRICK COLLINS

Lord's – Mecca for any cricket
follower with a Royal touch.
RICHARD HADLEE

You don't have to sit in the pavilion and watch
the slow compilation of centuries. If a side
gets thirty runs all told it will probably win.
S.P.B. MAIS

*On the first day,
Logie decided to chance
his arm and it came off.*
TREVOR BAILEY

So that's 57 runs needed by Hampshire in 11
overs and it doesn't need a calculator to tell you
that the run rate required is 5.1818.
NORMAN DeMESQUITA

I can't wait to get over here and
render my wife a cricket widow.
GEORGE SHEARING ON RETURNING
TO ENGLAND FOR HOLIDAYS

# *Yorkshire 232 all out, Hutton ill – I'm sorry, Hutton 111.*

JOHN SNAGGE

No captain with all the hindsight in the world
can predict how the wicket is going to play.
TREVOR BAILEY

It's a funny kind of month, October.
For the really keen cricket fan it's when you
discover that your wife left you in May.
DENIS NORDEN

It's a catch he would have
caught 99 times out of a 1000.
HENRY BLOFELD

# *Is there any sex in it?*

PETER SELLERS

Bill Frindal has done a bit of mental
arithmetic with a calculator.
JOHN ARLOTT

Anyone foolish enough to predict the
outcome of this match is a fool.
FRED TRUEMAN

If you go in with two fast bowlers and one
breaks down, you're left two short.
BOB MASSIE

The revolutionary notion of 'Middle England'
enjoying itself at a cricket match is
admittedly an alarming one.
DEREK BIRLEY

I must say, I'm rather fond of cricket,
though I wouldn't like anyone outside
this planet to hear me saying that.
DOUGLAS ADAMS

That's a remarkable catch by Yardley,
especially as the ball quite literally rolled
along the ground towards him.
MIKE DENNESS

*Boiley, you're
a statue, I wish
I was a pigeon.*
MELBOURNE SPECTATOR TO TREVOR BAILEY

Fair-minded people will know that the
umpire has a very small chance against
the odds of bowler and batsman.
TOM SMITH

The Queen's Park Oval, exactly as the name
suggests, absolutely round.
TONY COZIER

It's been a very slow and dull day, but it hasn't been
boring. It's been a good, entertaining day's cricket.
TONY BENNEWORTH

# *He caught it like shelling peas.*

FRED TRUEMAN

It's not in support of cricket but
as an earnest protest against golf.
MAX BEERBOHM ON SUBSCRIBING A
SHILLING TO W.G. GRACE'S TESTIMONIAL

The wicket was 'plumb', the batting orthodox,
and if there is anything more boring than
orthodox batting on a 'plumb' wicket
I suppose it is professional billiards.
A.P. HERBERT

We owe some gratitude to Gatting and
Lamb, who breathed some life into a
corpse which had nearly expired.
TREVOR BAILEY

# I don't think he expected it, and that's what caught him unawares.

TREVOR BAILEY

While I think you have a vulgar voice you have a compensatingly interesting mind.
S.J. LOTBINIERE INVITING JOHN ARLOTT TO COMMENTATE ON HIS FIRST OVERSEAS TOUR

And Ian Greig's on eight, including two fours.
JIM LAKER

Cricket is nothing if no one wants to watch it.
LORD MACLAURIN

53

... That was a 'photo-finish' and as there isn't
time to develop the plate, I shall say not out.

ALEC SKELDING

Once the authorities start tinkering with the
implements of the game, there is no telling
where supposed reforms will end.
C. STEWART CAINE

Six hundred million people take an interest in cricket.
Only 0.0001 per cent of them turn up to watch.
SIMON HUGHES

For any budding cricketers listening, do you have
any superstitious routines before an innings, like
putting one pad on first and then the other one?
TONY LEWIS

*Unless something
happens that we can't
predict, I don't think
a lot will happen.* FRED TRUEMAN

# *Beyond the Boundary*

In affectionate remembrance of English Cricket,
which died at the Oval on 29th August, 1882,
deeply lamented by a large circle of sorrowing
friends and acquaintances, R.I.P.
EPITAPH FROM THE *SPORTING TIMES*, 1882

Paid cricket players on Shrove-Tuesday, to
entertain the populace and to prevent the
infamous practice of throwing at cocks – 14s. 6d.
EXTRACT FROM THE 1757 ACCOUNTS
OF A LEEDS CHURCH

Parsons are not above giving very doubtful
decisions at the wicket in favour of their friends.
JOHN TREVISICK

I know plenty of professionals whom
I would delight to have as guests in my own
home, but I am afraid I cannot say the same
thing about many of the Australians.
A.W. CARR

*Never let your mind
go 'wool-gathering'
miles away from the
cricket field, or a
mistake is sure
to be made.*
DAVID DENTON

*Kent is emphatically the field of the cricketer's glory.*

JOHN MITFORD

I had the feeling that if Goebbels had been able to broadcast that the war had stopped cricket at Lord's it would have been invaluable propaganda for the Germans.

P. F. 'PLUM' WARNER

Looking backward we could almost see, suspended with the most delicate equipoise above the flat little island, the ghostly shapes of those twin orbs of the Empire, the cricket ball and the blackball.

PATRICK LEIGH FERMOR ON BARBADOS

It's called Behind the Crease and it's about the three things the English like most – sex, royalty and cricket – not necessarily in that order.

ERIC IDLE ON A RADIO PLAY HE WROTE WITH JOHN DU PRE

# *The Sri Lankan team have lost their heads, literally.*

GAMINE GOONASENA

I hold strongly to the opinion that the
toss, as an essential feature of cricket,
should not be tampered with.
SYDNEY PARDON: WISDEN'S EDITOR 1891–1925

Take care of your feet . . . Always have a spare
pair of socks to change into on leaving the field.
F.T. BADCOCK

My wife had an uncle who could never
walk down the nave of his abbey without
wondering where it would take a spin.
LORD HOME

The Editor of Wisden is an important personage.

P. F. 'PLUM' WARNER

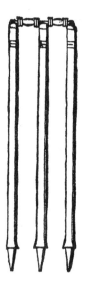

When ye first Wicket is pitched and ye popping
Crease cut, which must be exactly 3 foot 10 inches
from ye Wicket, ye other Wicket is to be pitched,
directly opposite, at 22 yeards distance, and ye other
popping Crease cut 3 foot 10 inches before it.

EXTRACT FROM 'THE GAME OF CRICKET
AS SETTLED BY YE CRICKET CLUB AT YE STAR
AND GARTER IN PALL MALL', 1755

'Memorandum, June ye 23rd, 1708.
Wee beat Ash Street at Creckits.'
EXTRACT FROM A KENTISH FARMER'S DIARY
IN THE BRITISH MUSEUM


Being a Yorkshireman, he had no time for any game
of cricket that did not resemble a full-scale war.
MICHAEL PARKINSON ON HIS FATHER

The ball must weigh not less than Five Ounces
and a Half, no more than Five Ounces
and Three Quarters.
THE LAWS OF CRICKET: AS REVISED BY THE
CRICKET CLUB, AT ST-MARY-LE-BONE, 1820

*Never read print,
it spoils one's eye
for the ball.*
W.G. GRACE

# It matters not who won or lost, but how you place the blame.

SIMON HUGHES

He brings to the fierce struggle of politics
the tepid enthusiasm of a lazy summer
afternoon at a cricket match.

ANEURIN BEVAN ON CLEMENT ATTLEE

61

In years to come it may be that the historian
will look upon the earlier seasons of the
twentieth century almost as a single summer.

ERIC PARKER

John Henry Newman was as English as roast beef,
even if he lacked a passion for cricket.

CLIFFORD LONGLEY

# It is sport's mental equivalent of being a Battle of Britain pilot.

MATTHEW ENGEL ON TEST-LEVEL UMPIRING

From the first the new scheme was a failure …
Those who planned the scheme had forgotten
that onlookers and players both want food.
ERIC PARKER ON THE POST-WORLD WAR I PLAN TO
LIMIT COUNTY CRICKET MATCHES TO TWO DAYS,
WITH PLAY ENDING AT HALF-PAST SEVEN

The Oxford and Cambridge boat race and cricket
match are the two anchors of the Universities in
the heart of the English people.
PROFESSOR CASE

For too long the county clubs have existed on a
diet of complacency and romanticism.

IAN BOTHAM

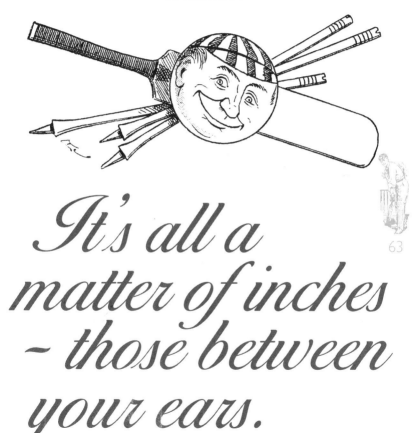

63

*It's all a
matter of inches
– those between
your ears.*

ARTHUR MILTON ON THE ART OF SPIN

If we give cricket to cable television it will
be game, set and match so far as the major
sporting events in Britain are concerned.
LORD ORME

As Hamlet is full of quotations,
so cricket is full of nostalgia . . .
KARL JOHNSTON

English spinners are like a necktie.
They add a spurious air of respectability
but perform no actual function.
SIMON BARNES

*Oh God, if there be
cricket in heaven,
let there also be*
ALEC DOUGLAS HOME *rain.*